Library of Congress Cataloging-in-Publication Data

Field, Eugene, 1850-1895.
Wynken, Blynken, and Nod / by Eugene W. Field; illustrated by David McPhail.
p. cm.
"Cartwheel Books."
Summary: A classic lullaby poem about three fishermen who try to catch the stars in nets of silver and gold.
ISBN 0-439-54303-7
 1. Children's poetry, American. 2. Sleep—Juvenile poetry. [1. Sleep—Poetry. 2. American poetry.] I. McPhail, David, 1940- ill. II.Title.
PS1667 .W8 2004
811'.4—dc21   2003007706

10 9 8 7 6 5 4 3 2 1   04 05 06 07 08

Printed in Singapore 46 • First printing, January 2004

Wynken, Blynken, and Nod

Written by Eugene W. Field
Illustrated by David McPhail

Cartwheel
B·O·O·K·S ®

SCHOLASTIC INC.

New York Toronto London Auckland Sydney
Mexico City New Delhi Hong Kong Buenos Aires

Wynken, Blynken, and Nod one night

Sailed off in a wooden shoe—

Sailed on a river of crystal light,

Into a sea of dew.

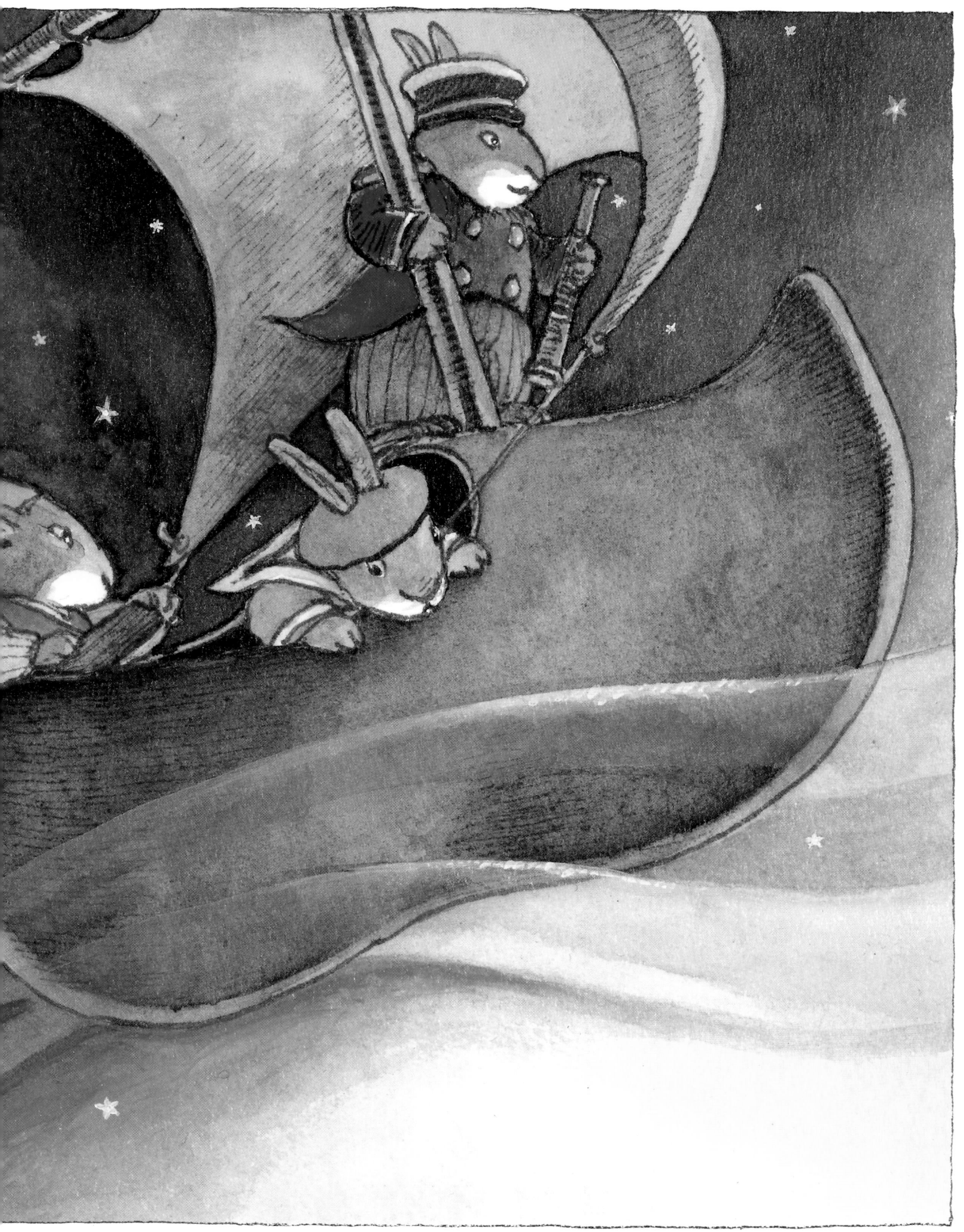

"Where are you going,

And what do you wish?"

The old moon

Asked the three.

"We have come to fish

For the herring fish

That live in this beautiful sea;

Nets of silver and gold have we,"

Said Wynken, Blynken, and Nod.

The old moon laughed and sang a song,

As they rocked in the wooden shoe,

And the wind that sped them all night long

Ruffled the waves of dew.

The little stars were the herring fish

That lived in that beautiful sea;

"Now cast your nets wherever you wish,

Never afeard are we!"

So cried the stars to the fishermen three,

Wynken,

Blynken,

And Nod.

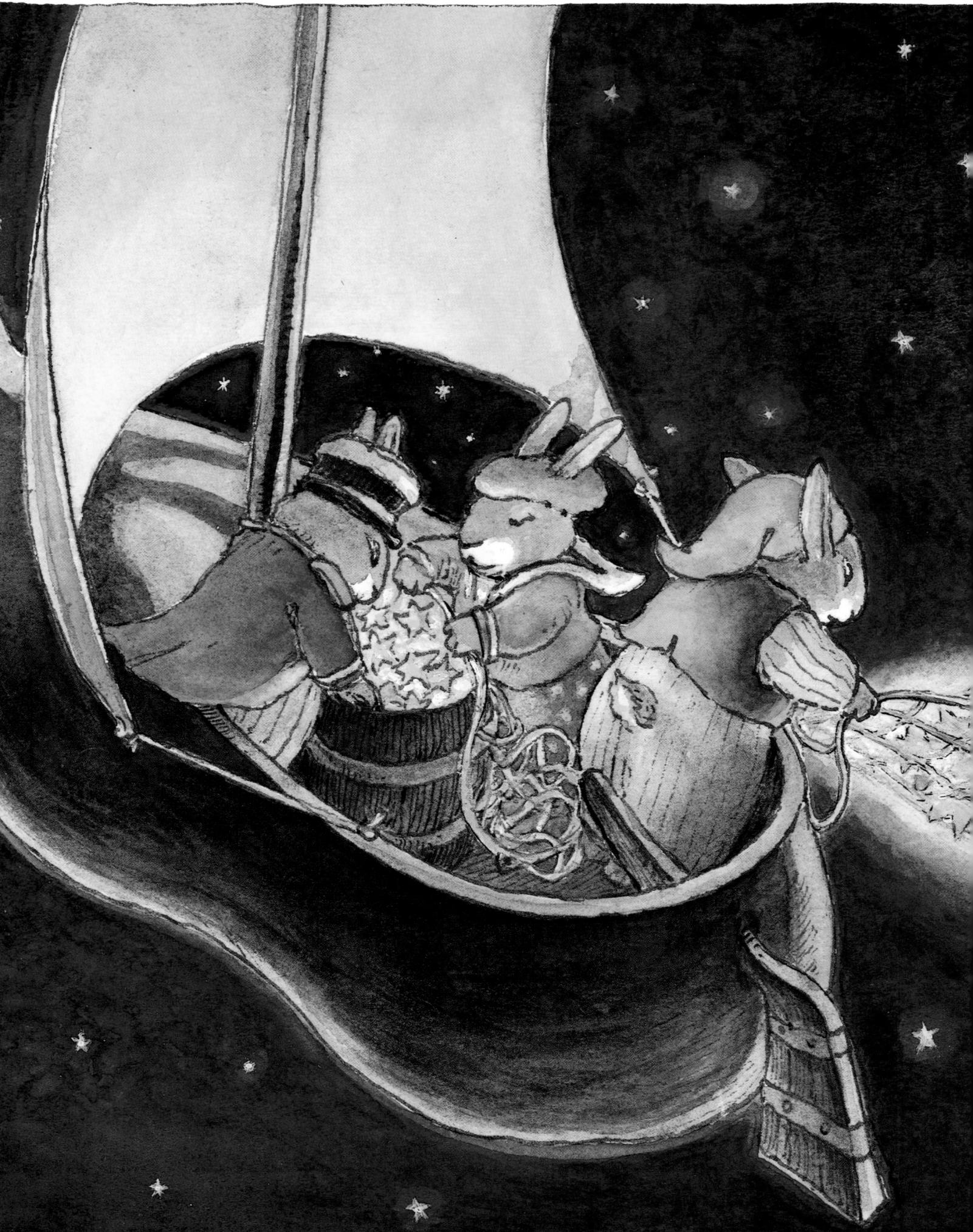

All night long their nets they threw

To the stars in the twinkling foam;

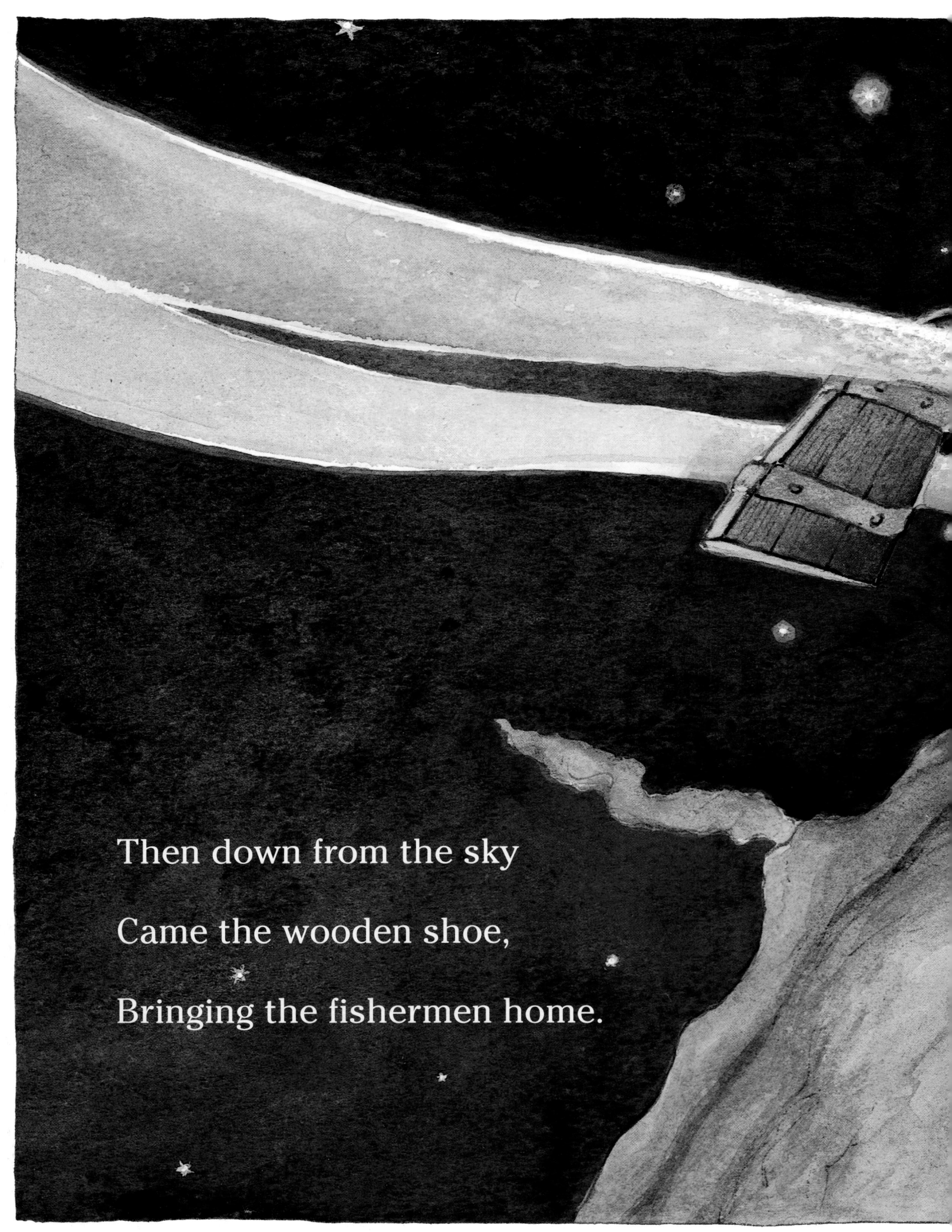

Then down from the sky

Came the wooden shoe,

Bringing the fishermen home.

'Twas all so pretty a sail,

It seemed as if it could not be;

And some folk thought

'Twas a dream they'd dreamed

Of sailing that beautiful sea.

But I shall name you

The fishermen three,

Wynken, Blynken, and Nod.

Wynken and Blynken are two little eyes,

And Nod is a little head,

And the wooden shoe that sailed the skies

Is a wee one's trundle bed.

So shut your eyes while Mother sings

Of wonderful sights that be,

And you shall see the beautiful things

As you rock in the misty sea,

Where the old shoe rocked

The fishermen three,

Wynken,

Blynken,

And Nod.

On March 9, 1889, Eugene W. Field created *Wynken, Blynken, and Nod.* "The little story occurred to me as I was riding home on the streetcars," he once said. Although Mr. Field had intended to write a "windmill story," when he thought of the names Wynken, Blynken, and Nod, he "took up with the wooden shoe." He said, "I sat up in bed and wrote out the lullaby as it now appears, with the exception that I first wrote, 'Into a sea of blue,' and this line I changed to, 'Into a sea of dew.'" The original version of this poem was written on brown wrapping paper.